ISBN 978-0-9892912-8-6

Boyack, Connor, author.
Stanfield, Elijah, illustrator.
The Tuttle Twins and the Miraculous Pencil / Connor Boyack.

Cover design by Elijah Stanfield
Edited and typeset by Connor Boyack

Printed in the United States

THE TUTTLE TWINS
— and the —
MIRACULOUS
PENCIL

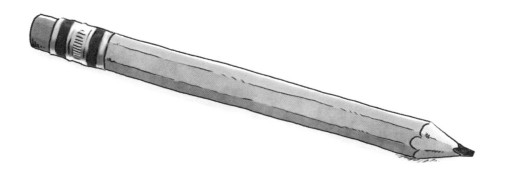

CONNOR BOYACK

Illustrated by Elijah Stanfield

This book is dedicated to
Leonard Read (1898-1983).

Thanks for giving a voice
to the pencil.

Ethan and Emily Tuttle had been looking forward to their class field trip for weeks. They loved experiencing new things—especially when they got to leave school for the morning!

Mrs. Miner, the twins' teacher, had been helping her students understand what an *economy* is.

She taught them that an economy is just a fancy word for lots of people working together to buy and sell things. To learn more about it, Mrs. Miner decided to take the class on a field trip to a place where people make things to sell to others.

She even let the students choose where they should go. They came up with several suggestions: a restaurant, a farm, a computer company, and a bakery (fresh cinnamon rolls sounded great!). After a long discussion, the class settled on a different idea.

They decided they would visit a factory where
the workers make things that students use, such
as pens, pencils, notebooks, and rulers. Mrs. Miner
hinted that they might even get a souvenir!

When the bus arrived at the factory, the kids were a little disappointed. It was nothing like they imagined.

One of the kids groaned, "This looks boring! There's no way anything fun happens here." Another complained, "I wish we went to the cinnamon roll bakery instead!"

"Don't worry kids," Mrs. Miner said. "The magic happens inside!"

They all shuffled inside and walked past a large room
full of machines. One of the workers waved to them.
The kids all stopped and pushed their noses up
against the glass to get a better look.

"Look at all that paper!" shouted Ethan, pointing
through the window at large rolls of paper that looked
as big as their school bus.

"C'mon everybody," said Mrs. Miner. "I bet we'll get a
better look at those machines a little later."

9

The students were led to a room where a friendly man greeted them, handing each of them a pencil.

"Welcome, everybody!" the man said. "My name is Carl, and I work here. Can all of you do me a favor and hold up the pencil I gave you?"

They each held up their pencil. Emily stretched hers high into the air, twirling it between her fingers with the hope of being noticed.

"Here's my question for you as we begin today," said Carl. "Do you think the pencil you're holding is easy or hard to make?"

A couple of the kids quickly said "easy!" and then everybody else said the same thing, copying the students who had answered first.

"Well I'm going to make a bold claim," Carl said as he smiled. "That pencil in your hands is actually extremely difficult to make, and surprisingly enough, not a single person on the face of this earth knows how to make one!"

Ethan and Emily looked at each other with looks of disbelief on their faces.

"That's impossible!" shouted a girl named Jessica. "Then how can there be any pencils if nobody knows how to make them?"

"That's a great question!" replied Carl. "Let me come back to that after we talk a little more." He then turned around and drew a bunch of lines on the whiteboard.

"This is kind of like a family tree, which lets us see all of the people who help make us who we are—our parents, our grandparents, and so on."

"Look at that pencil in your hands," he said. "What are the parts that make up a pencil, and where did they all come from? What is the pencil's family tree?"

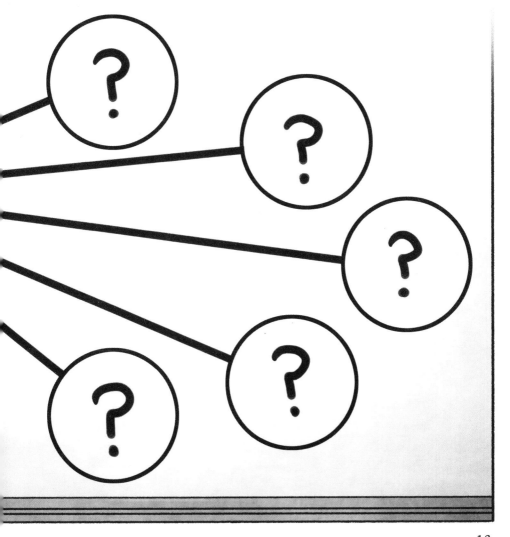

"Wood!" shouted Ethan excitedly. His classmates joined in to provide a list of other pieces: lead, an eraser, some metal to hold the eraser to the pencil, and some paint. Carl wrote them down.

"Great! Now, I need a volunteer. How about you?" he asked, pointing to Emily. "I want you to try and continue this chart. Start with the wood—where does it come from?"

Emily stood up and wrote *tree* in one of the circles of the family tree. "And how does the tree get from the forest to the factory?" Carl asked.

"Well, some people would have to cut it down," Emily said. "And then they would have to put it on a truck." She then wrote *saw* and *truck* on the family tree.

"Let's keep it going," said Carl, as Emily sat down. "What materials would a person need to be able to make a truck?"

Ethan's hand shot up. "You would need fuel, so it could run. And lots of metal. And rubber for the tires. You'd also need rope to tie the logs to the truck," he said as Carl wrote them on the board.

"Does anybody here know how to make rope?" Carl asked. Nobody raised their hand. "Think of all the hemp plants that need to be grown to make it—and the equipment used to water those plants, and the machines built to harvest them."

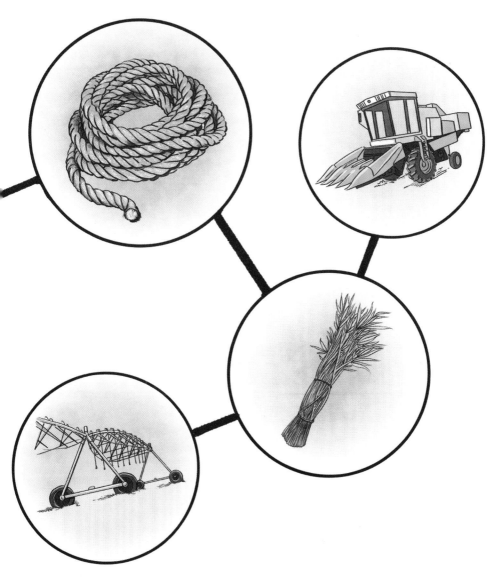

"And all of these workers need to eat, right?" Carl continued. "We can't work without eating, so we have to also think of the farmers, the grocery store employees, and the cooks."

"We need all those things to make a pencil?" one of the students asked.

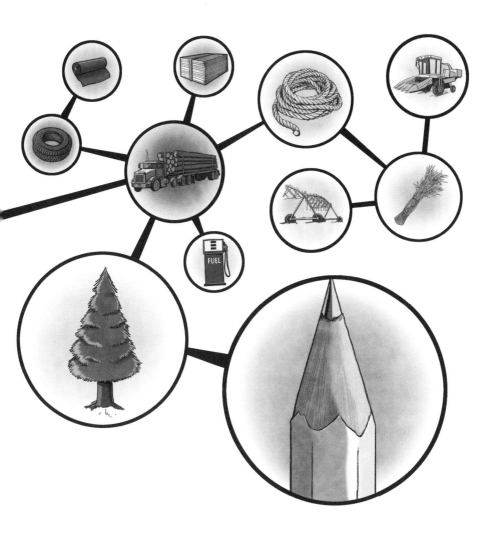

"Nope, we need all those things—and many more—just to get the wood for the pencil!" Carl said with a chuckle.

The students were amazed. Now they were beginning to understand that making a simple pencil was not so simple at all.

"Now let's learn about the other parts of the pencil's family tree," Carl said.

Carl started a video chat with a smiling woman who waved to the children. "This is Mary, everybody. She's in charge of buying the best materials from all over the world for us to use."

"Wow, where are you, Mary?" asked Emily.

"Well, I usually work in London," she responded. "But today I'm in South Korea to inspect some graphite we want to buy to make pencil lead."

"What's so special about South Korea?" Carl asked her. "Why don't we buy it somewhere else?"

"That's an important question," Mary said. "We want to sell our pencils at a low price, so we have to find the best materials at the least expensive prices— wherever that might be."

"This means that people all around the world compete for our business!" she said.

Mary explained how the graphite they purchase is mined in a large, open pit, and then heated and compressed in a processing plant. The graphite is then packaged and shipped to another factory to be mixed with clay, wax, and chemicals.

"I visit many places around the world, buying different materials to make our pencils. The yellow paint, called lacquer, is made from castor oil which comes from plants grown in India," Mary said.

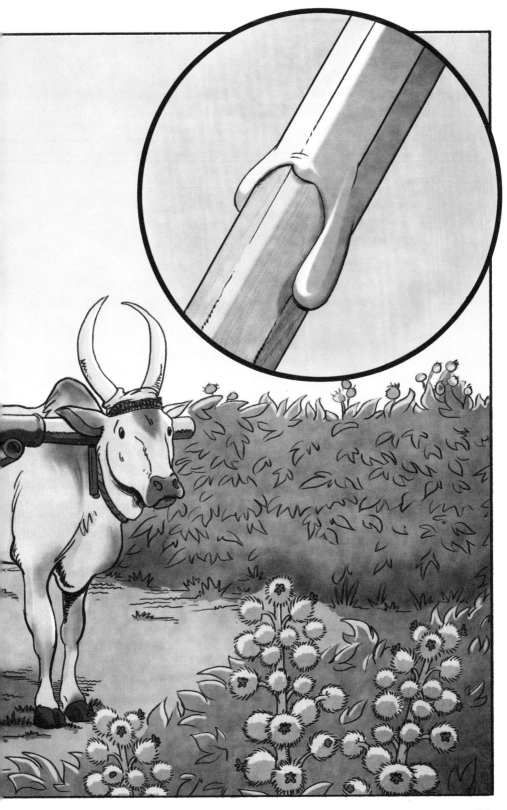

"To make our erasers, we buy rapeseed oil from Indonesia and oil from rubber trees grown in Africa. We also use pumice from Italy to make them gritty, so they work better," she added.

"The ferrule is the small piece of metal
that helps secure the eraser to the pencil,"
Mary explained. "We cut them out from sheets
of brass we buy from people who mine the zinc
and copper ore. They melt the metals, mix them
together, and press them into sheets for us to use."

"Each step in the process requires big machines and many people from all around the world working together," said Carl. "The different parts are finally shipped to us, and we put them all together to make a pencil."

The kids waved goodbye to Mary as Carl led them to where they could see the factory floor.

Ethan craned his neck to better see everything below. He could see the wood pieces being cut, glued, and attached around the long, skinny pieces of graphite.

A large machine was also spraying the yellow lacquer onto each of the pencils, and another was attaching the eraser with tiny ferrules.

Emily closely inspected every part of the pencil she was holding. It was so interesting to think about all the people who had worked together to make it, and how the different parts came from all over the world!

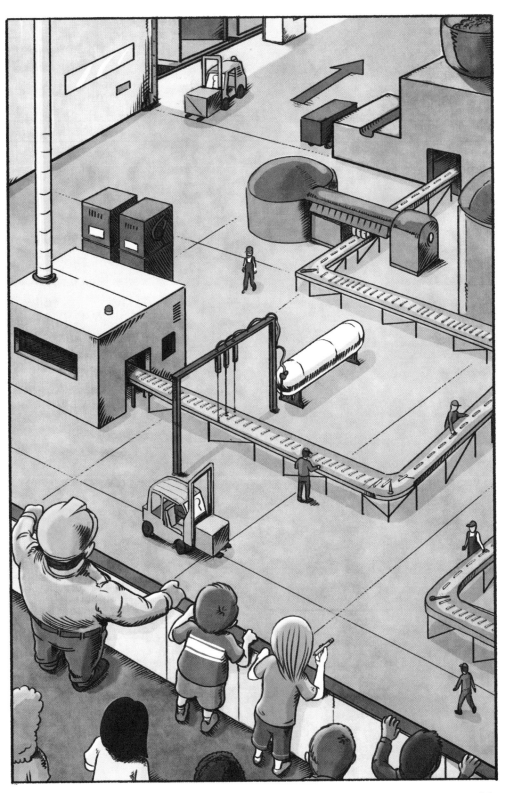

After returning to their room, Carl directed everybody's attention to the whiteboard. "If we were to write a pencil's entire family tree, it would be very, *very* large," he said.

Ethan was trying to remember all the things involved in making a pencil, but there were so many that he lost count and forgot some of them.

"Remember what you asked earlier, young lady?" Carl asked Jessica. "You wanted to know how there can be pencils if nobody knows how to make them. Do you know now?"

"I think it's because nobody knows how to make all the different parts of a pencil all by themselves," she replied.

"That's right!" Carl said. "If you tried to make a pencil without anyone else helping you, it would be impossible."

"How could you travel all over the world to get the materials you needed without ships or planes?" he asked the kids.

"How would you gather each of the materials without tools and machines? Or put them together without factories?" Carl asked.

"And if you were busy doing all of that, when would you have time to find food to eat, or build a home to live in?"

Carl stretched his arms out to say, "That's why it takes millions of people working together—people who don't speak the same language, who practice different religions, who live in different countries, and who will never even meet one another."

"Do all those people even know they're making a pencil?" wondered Ethan aloud.

"No, they don't," replied Carl. "Let's think of it a different way. What type of work would you like to do when you grow up?"

The kids shouted out their answers, including a house builder, a teacher, a musician, a farmer, an astronaut, and a scientist. Ethan wanted to be a basketball player, and Emily said she wanted to be a doctor!

"The logger who cuts down trees for the pencils doesn't know if the wood will be turned into furniture, a house, a pencil, or something else," Carl responded. "He may not even like using pencils!"

"The same is true for the doctor who might treat the logger and his family, the farmer who feeds the doctor, or even the musician who entertains the farmer," he added. "Almost every job you can think of may actually be helping to make a part of the pencil without the person even realizing it."

"And that's how it works for everything that's made, right?" Emily asked. "Not just pencils?"

"Definitely," Carl said. "Your clothes, your backpacks, your shoes—everything you own and use requires many people working together."

"Remember," added Mrs. Miner, "the economy is made up of people buying and selling things. If people tried to make everything on their own, they wouldn't be able to and life would be hard."

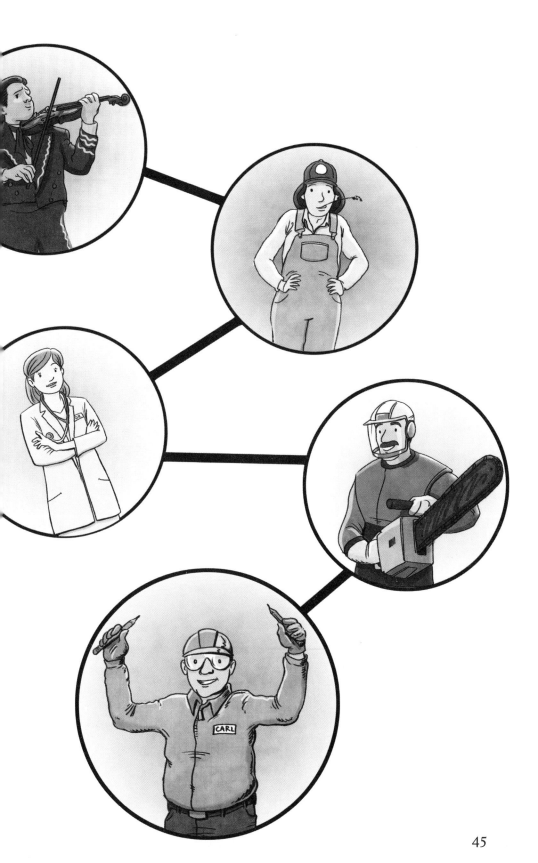

"But because we divide up the work into different jobs, each person works on something that others can use," she said. "We work together automatically, without even really knowing it. There's no boss telling everybody what to do."

This is something we call *spontaneous order*, and it's the reason why we can have so many wonderful things today!" said Mrs. Miner.

"It's time for you to head home now," said Carl. "But before you go, take another look at your new pencil."

"Millions of people, including me, helped make your pencil—but we don't know how you will use it. Will your pencil draw plans for a new invention? Will it make a work of art? Will it help you do your homework, or write a letter?"

"The pencil's family tree continues with each of you, and it will continue on and on for as long as you keep making new things with it."

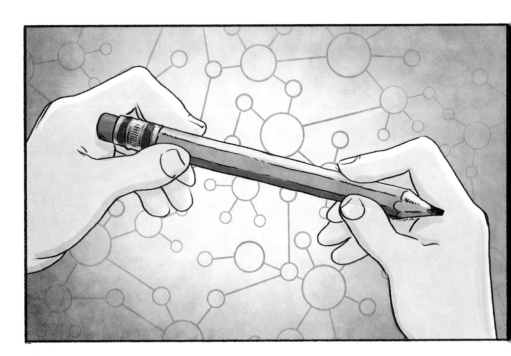

Carl waved goodbye to each of the students. "I hope you do something great with your pencils!" he shouted as they loaded back onto the bus.

"So what did you all learn about today?" asked Donald, the bus driver.

Mrs. Miner, with a smile on her face, quickly answered. "They all learned how to make pencils, right everybody?"

The kids laughed, and Ethan shouted "I don't know how to make a pencil, Mrs. Miner. Nobody does!"

For the rest of the trip home, Ethan and Emily took turns looking through their backpacks wondering about how all of the miraculous objects were made.

It was like a new world had been opened up to them, imagining the entire family tree of everything they saw!

The End

The Author

Connor Boyack is president of Libertas Institute, a free market think tank in Utah. In that capacity he has changed a significant number of laws in favor of personal freedom and free markets, and has launched a variety of educational projects, including The Tuttle Twins children's book series. Connor is the author of over a dozen books.

A California native and Brigham Young University graduate, Connor currently resides in Lehi, Utah, with his wife and two children.

The Illustrator

Elijah Stanfield is owner of Red House Motion Imaging, a media production company in Washington.

A longtime student of Austrian economics, history, and the classical liberal philosophy, Elijah has dedicated much of his time and energy to promoting the ideas of free markets and individual liberty. Some of his more notable works include producing eight videos in support of Ron Paul's 2012 presidential candidacy. He currently resides in Richland, Washington, with his wife April and their six children.

Contact us at TuttleTwins.com!

Glossary of Terms

Central planning: Control and regulation of the masses by a limited number of people using government to enforce their decisions and alter the behavior of other individuals.

Competition: Multiple producers or service providers trying to attract more customers by lowering their price, improving their product or service, or otherwise setting themselves apart.

Economy: A network of individuals who produce, distribute, and use goods and services.

Division of labor: A production process involving many different people, each of whom specialize in and work on a different task, thereby collaborating to do something greater together than any one of them could do alone.

Spontaneous order: When social harmony and market efficiency are achieved through the independent decisions of countless individuals, each guided by their own desires and self-interest.

Discussion Questions

1. Why is the economy important?
2. Would it be a good or bad idea to have a few people tell everybody else how to make or do something? Why?
3. Pick an object nearby—what does its family tree look like?
4. How has your life been improved by the division of labor?
5. Is there anything that you could make entirely on your own?

Don't Forget the Activity Workbook!

Visit **TuttleTwins.com/PencilWorkbook** to download the PDF and provide your children with all sorts of activities to reinforce the lessons they learned in the book!